Y YES! SAY YES! SAY YES! SAY YES! SAY YES! SAY YES! SAY YES! SAY Y
YES! SAY YES! SAY YES! SAY YES! SAY YES! SAY YES! SAY YES! SAY YES

AY YES! SAY YES! SAY YES! SAY YES! SAY YES! SAY YES! SAY YES! SAY YES! SAY
YES! SAY YES! SAY YES! SAY YES! SAY YES! SAY YES! SAY YES! SA

SAY

SAY

YES!

BY R. PAUL FIRNHABER

YES!

Published by
Concordia Publishing House, St. Louis, Missouri
Concordia Publishing House Ltd., London, E. C. 1

Library of Congress Catalog Card No. 68-25511
MANUFACTURED IN THE UNITED STATES OF AMERICA

THIS IS A NON-BOOK.

IT MIGHT BE CALLED A COLLAGE. OR A MOSAIC.

IT PLAYS FREELY WITH VERBAL/VISUAL IMAGES, DEMANDING ATTENTION, INVOLVEMENT, RESPONSE.

IT'S MORE LIKE WATCHING TV OR WALKING DOWN A BUSY STREET THAN READING A BOOK.

IT JOURNEYS INTO THE WORLD OF TAKEN-FOR-GRANTEDNESSES, SEARCHING THEM FOR THE POSSIBILITY OF NEW MEANINGS.

IT TALKS ABOUT A REALITY THAT EXISTS AMONG US, SEEN ONLY BY THE EYES OF FAITH.

IT INSISTS THAT ADS, FOOD, PEOPLE, WORDS, HEADLINES, SAYINGS, EVENTS, MAGAZINES, AND TV TUBES SAY MORE THAN IS IMMEDIATELY APPARENT.

IT CLAIMS THAT THE INCARNATION, ESPECIALLY AS EXPRESSED IN THE EUCHARIST, DEMANDS A NEW LOOK AT LIFE AND THE WORLD.

IT SHOUTS OUT IN NO UNCERTAIN TERMS THAT GOD IS ALIVE IN THE WORLD AND THAT THE WHOLE CREATION EXISTS AS AN INTENDED SIGN OF THAT PRESENCE.

IT CAN'T SIMPLY BE READ. OR ITS PICTURES SIMPLY LOOKED AT. IT'S GOT TO BE EXPERIENCED. AND MORE THAN ONCE. OR EVEN TWICE.

IT'S INTENDED TO PUSH YOU OUT INTO YOUR WORLD WITH SENSORS A BIT MORE TUNED TO WHAT'S REALLY HAPPENING.

IT SAYS YES TO GOD'S GIFT OF A WORLD.

IT ASKS YOU TO DO THE SAME.

HEAVEN AND EARTH WEREN'T MEANT TO BE A WORLD APART

THEY MEET IN BIRTH A CHILD IS BORN INTO THE WORLD we say IT COMES AS A GIFT OF GOD good

AND THEN A MAN IS TAKEN FROM THIS EARTH that's how it usually goes GOD AND MAN HEAVEN AND EARTH ONCE MORE BECOME ONE complete

ncing

ration

e new

dependabl

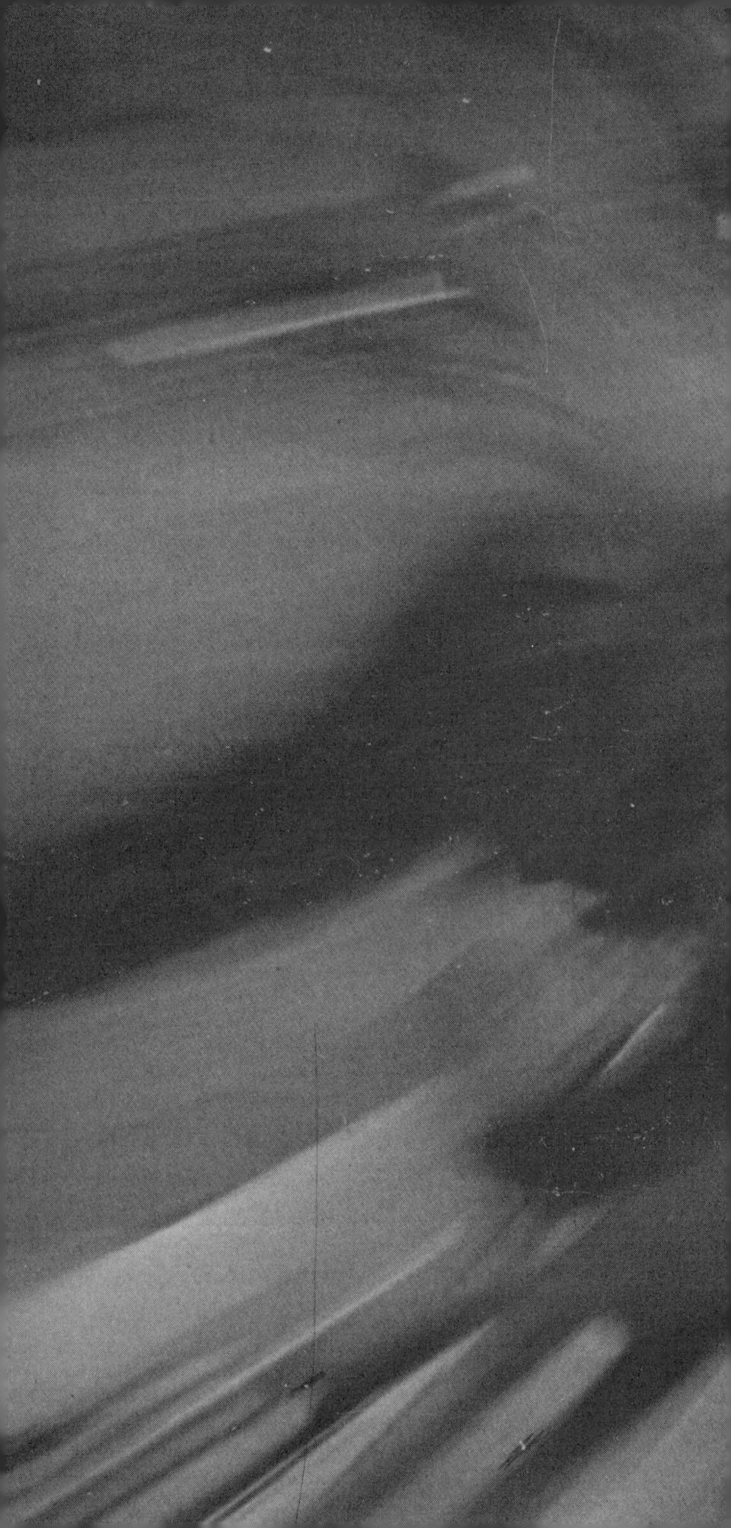

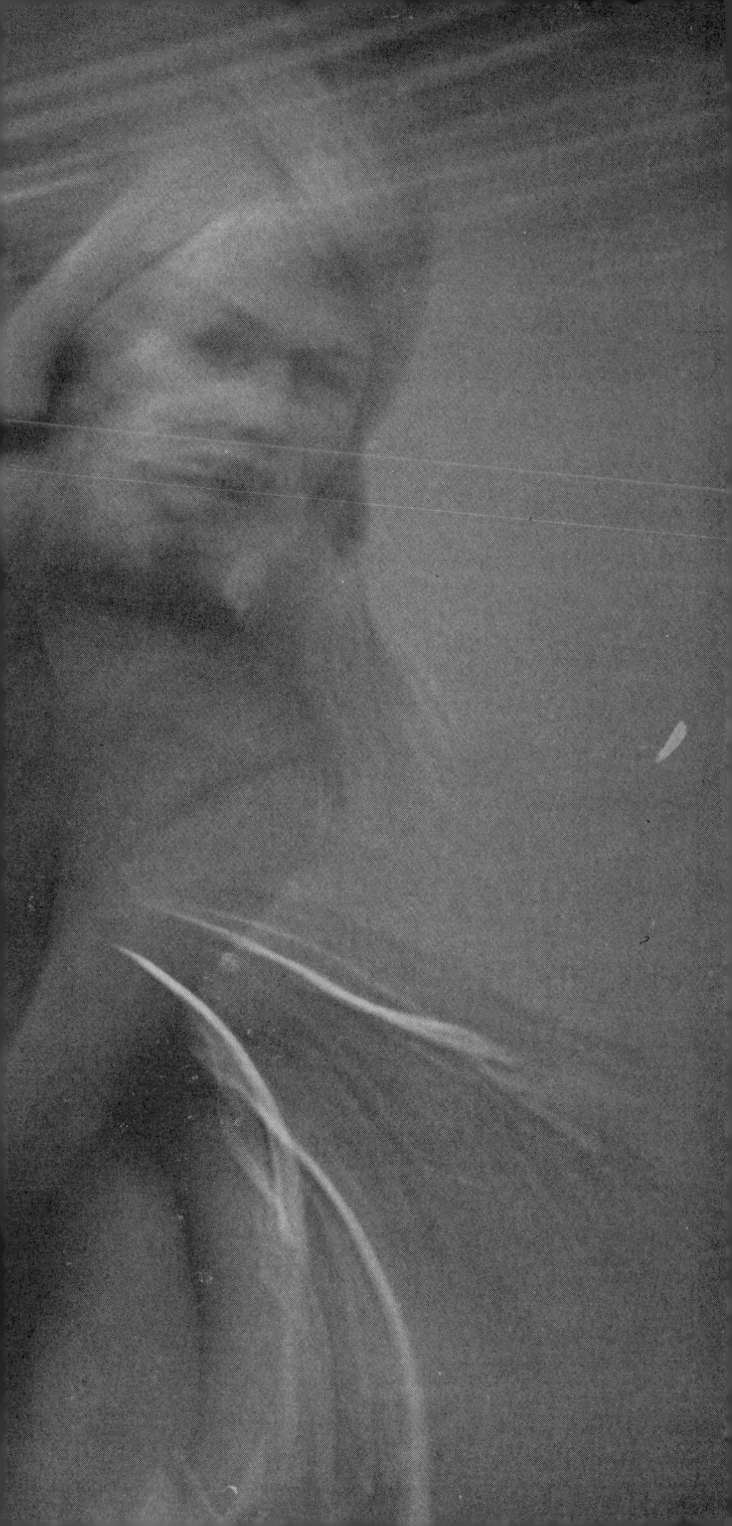

There are 30,000,000 people in this country aged 10 to 17.

They have funny haircuts.

They buy two and one half billion gallons of gasoline a year.

They worry about their complexions.

14% of them own corporate stocks and bonds.

They fall in love all the time.

The girls alone buy more than 20% of all women's clothes; the boys alone buy 40% of the slacks and 33% of the sweaters. Together they buy more than 35% of all sportswear.

They are mysteries to their mothers and fathers.

They are estimated to buy 20% of all cars sold.

Their mothers and fathers are mysteries to them.

They account for 44% of all camera sales, 55% of all soft drink sales, 35% of the movie audience.

They stay up too late, and wake up too early.

The girls buy 33% of all hairdryers, 23% of all cosmetics, spend over 20 million dollars on lipstick alone.

The boys spend a lot of time on looking at the girls. Someday they'll get married, and go on using the products that are getting to be habits now.

And we've got more of them with us than any other single medium.

Tell you what:

LIFE

BUT BETWEEN BIRTH AND DEATH THE MEETINGS OF HEAVEN AND EARTH from our view ARE TOO FEW AND FAR BETWEEN

Buy our
10 million teenagers
and we'll throw in
our 33 million adults
for free.

WATER

MEL

A TIME few minutes hours SET ASIDE now and then
DAILY WEEKLY YEARLY

ONE PLACE IN A THOUSAND dedicated and NAMED
A SANCTUARY from what for what

AN EVENT SPECIALLY RECALLED

OR ONE JUST HAPPENING WHERE IT IS almost
IMPOSSIBLE NOT TO SEE GOD AT WORK

BUT ONLY A GLIMPSE here A GRAB there here A BIT
there A HINT MUCH TOO INFREQUENTLY to say the
least

AND LIFE'S TOO HARD FOR THAT

SO WE LEARN too bad TO LIVE BY AND FOR THOSE
SPECIAL extra TIMES PLACES EVENTS PEOPLE
THINGS HAPPENINGS

WE LEARN TO BOUNCE ALONG FROM ONE SUMMIT
TO ANOTHER MANAGING THE VOIDS BETWEEN
ONLY BECAUSE ANOTHER SUMMIT IS SIGHTED ON
THE HORIZON OR ONE STILL VISIBLE IN THE
REARVIEW MIRROR

Go ahead, whistle.

He won't come.

Loo

FROM BIRTHDAY TO PROM GRID VICTORY TO CAGE VICTORY MIDTERM B TO FINAL A—

breath bated

NOT FREE TO EXHALE TILL ANOTHER IS WITHIN EASY REACH   aaahhhhhh

AND WHILE THEY ARE HAPPENING WE WALLOW IN THEM LIKE WE WEREN'T MEANT TO DO ANYTHING ELSE UNDER THE SUN BUT CELEBRATE

t *all* you get yo

u can't get any

the

BUT FOR SOME stupid REASON CONTENT AND SATISFIED do we have a choice TO BELIEVE THAT THE SPACES BETWEEN HIGH TIMES GREAT PEOPLE SPECIAL PLACES AND GOOD THINGS

DESERVE ONLY TO BE PUT UP WITH what a drag

where else!

twic

ONE WOULD THINK if he thought hard enough THAT THERE WOULD BE A WAY surely not a simple one THAT IN OUR MAJOR and even minor CELEBRATINGS ONE somehow COULD MAKE WAVES

BIG ENOUGH TO LAP OVER at least a little bit INTO THE THIRSTY AND LESS LIGHTED CREVICES AND CRANNIES the spaces between

SO THAT GOOD TIMES AREN'T JUST USED TO PROPEL US TO OTHER GOOD TIMES admitting that the spaces between are less than good

LIVING BY AND FOR SPECIALS ISN'T ENOUGH

SOMEHOW one would think SPECIALS SHOULD BE SEEN TO EXIST FOR THE REGULARS

AND THE REGULARS FOR THE SPECIALS

IS IT A POSSIBILITY

GOOD NEWS AS DAILY NEWS AND DAILY NEWS AS GOOD NEWS

NOT just CERTAIN THINGS say things with special historic value or things with holy shapes BUT ALL GOD'S THINGS AS GOOD AND WORTHY

Stop reading like they did 100 years ago.

Just because we have a new look...

Don't think we haven't been around

Wet is because you're thirsty.

without the Wild you can't have the Wet

Wild is because you're you

Make up your mind

ALL MEN NOT JUST SOME AS VALUABLE

ALL TIME TIMES NOT JUST A FEW AS HIGH TIMES GOOD TIMES

THIS DOESN'T SAY THAT SOME TIMES OR PLACES OR PEOPLE OR EVENTS AREN'T SPECIAL SPECIAL

MAYBE WHAT HAPPENS IS THAT THE WHOLE BIT IS RAISED A NOTCH or so

SO THAT WE NOW HAVE SPECIAL AND SPECIAL SPECIAL HAPPENINGS INSTEAD OF JUST REGULAR AND SPECIAL

SPECIAL EDITION LIFE

AND A FEW VOLUMES here and there SPECIAL DELUXE EDITIONS

THEY DO IT WITH TOOTHPASTE AND DETERGENT WHO SELLS these days SMALL MEDIUM LARGE

CHEER IS REGULAR GIANT AND KING AND SO IS FAB AND BOLD

GLEEM AND ULTRA BRITE ARE likewise SUPER CAST

WHY CAN'T PEOPLE AND ALL COME SUPERLATIVELY

What's new at the supermarket, lady?

Do
you measure
your morning
paper in
width
or in depth?

AS IF ha HEAVEN AND EARTH WEREN'T SO FAR APART imagine

AS IF yes GOD HIMSELF superlative everything we were taught WAS REALLY PRESENT somehow

HIDDEN YES

BUT AMONG AND BETWEEN AND IN REGULAR PEOPLE EVENTS TIMES AND PLACES MAKING THEM SPECIAL just BECAUSE HE'S THERE

RECOGNIZABLE AND KNOWABLE TO THOSE WHO WANT TO SEE AND KNOW

HE WHO HAS EYES ears TO SEE hear LET HIM SEE hear

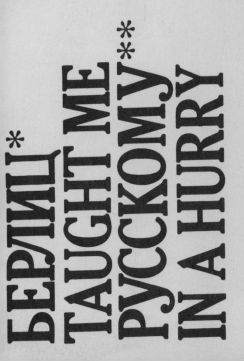

БЕРЛИЦ* TAUGHT ME РУССКОМУ** IN A HURRY

The critics are panning us

MAYBE THAT'S WHAT WE HAVE TO LEARN soon THAT WE DON'T HAVE TO somehow BRING GOD TO THINGS even people BUT INSTEAD CONVINCED THAT HE'S ALREADY PRESENT promises promises promises SAY YES AND CELEBRATE HIS PRESENCE

THERE HAVE ALWAYS BEEN SOME PEOPLE WHO FOUND WAYS OF DOING THAT SORT OF THING imperfectly

THEY'RE NOT ALWAYS REMEMBERED these people
OR EVEN RECOGNIZED invariably THEY'RE LITTLE
PEOPLE COMMON RUN OF THE MILL REGULAR
EVERYDAY SORTS

FEW WHEELS ATTAIN SAINTHOOD

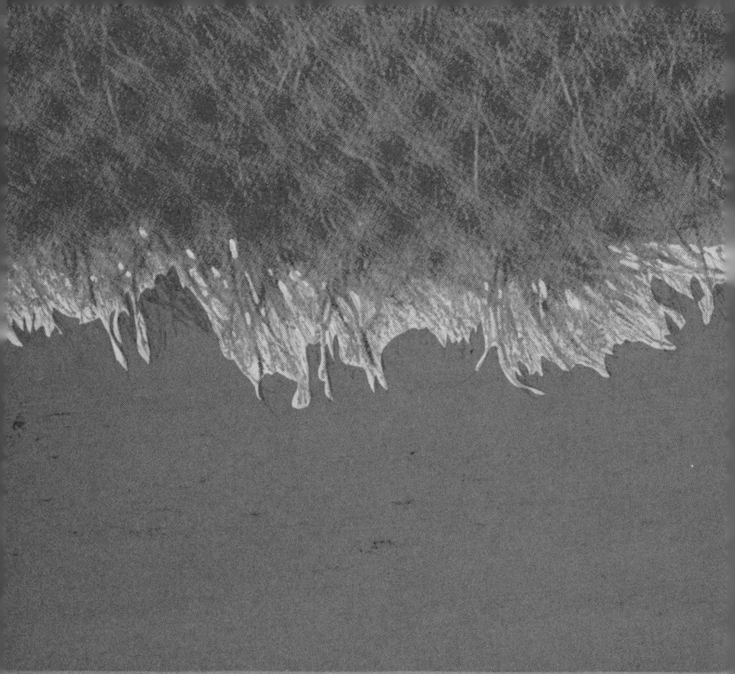

Taste is the name of the game

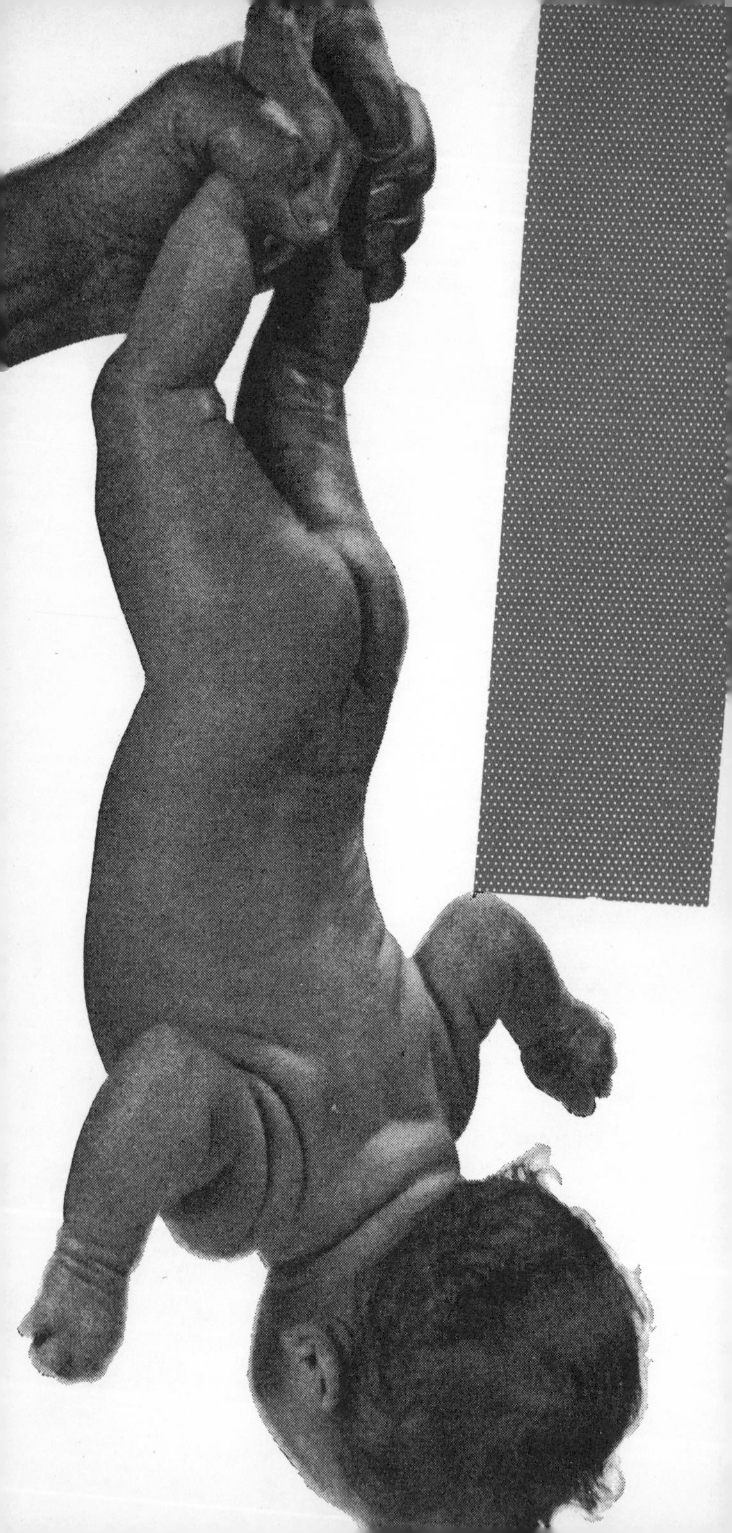

IN FACT IT SEEMS TO TAKE SPECIAL HISTORIES TO LOCATE THEM MOST PASS THEM BY or if they are remembered it was for something else

THEY GROW BEST IN BUNCHES it seems COMMON PEOPLE WITH THINGS IN COMMON COMMUNITIES MAY BE THE WORD it comes from common

‘What will I see on the moon?’

ONE SUCH BUNCH NEVER SEEMED TO DIE IN ANCIENT ISRAEL mideast mediterranean seacoast HEBREWS THEY WERE CALLED jews

AN UNCANNY WAY THEY HAD or at least a handful of them OF REMEMBERING WHO WHAT WHEN WHERE WHY THEY WERE BY REMEMBERING EVENTS IN THEIR HISTORY OR PLACES OR THINGS OR PEOPLE or whatever

CELEBRATING THEIR KINGSIZEDNESS BY DECLARING such audacity THAT GOD YAHWEH WAS BEHIND IT ALL all of it

THEY FINALLY BROKE OUT OF THAT EGYPTIAN BRICK FACTORY AND INSISTED THAT YAHWEH LED the civil rights march

THEY FINALLY FOUND SWEET WATER TO QUENCH THEIR DESERT THIRST AND THANKED YAHWEH it was a miracle

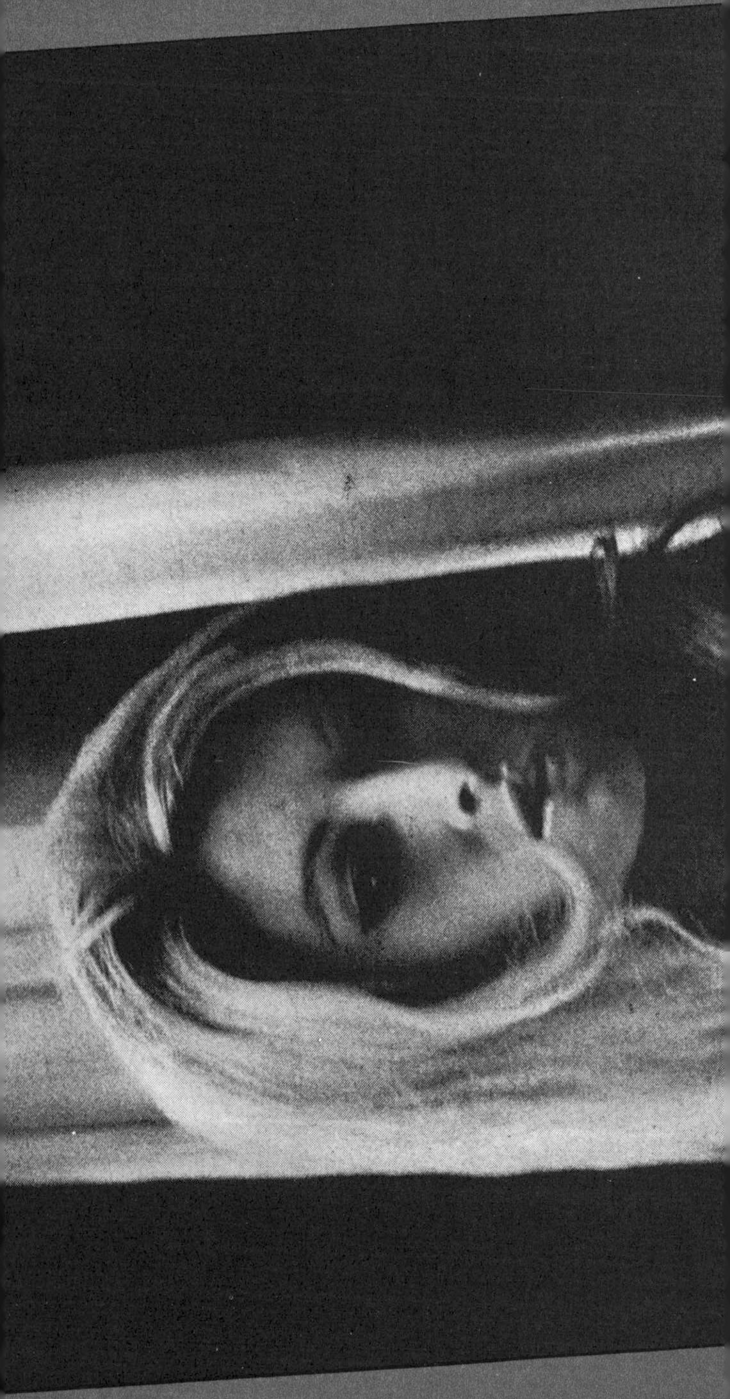

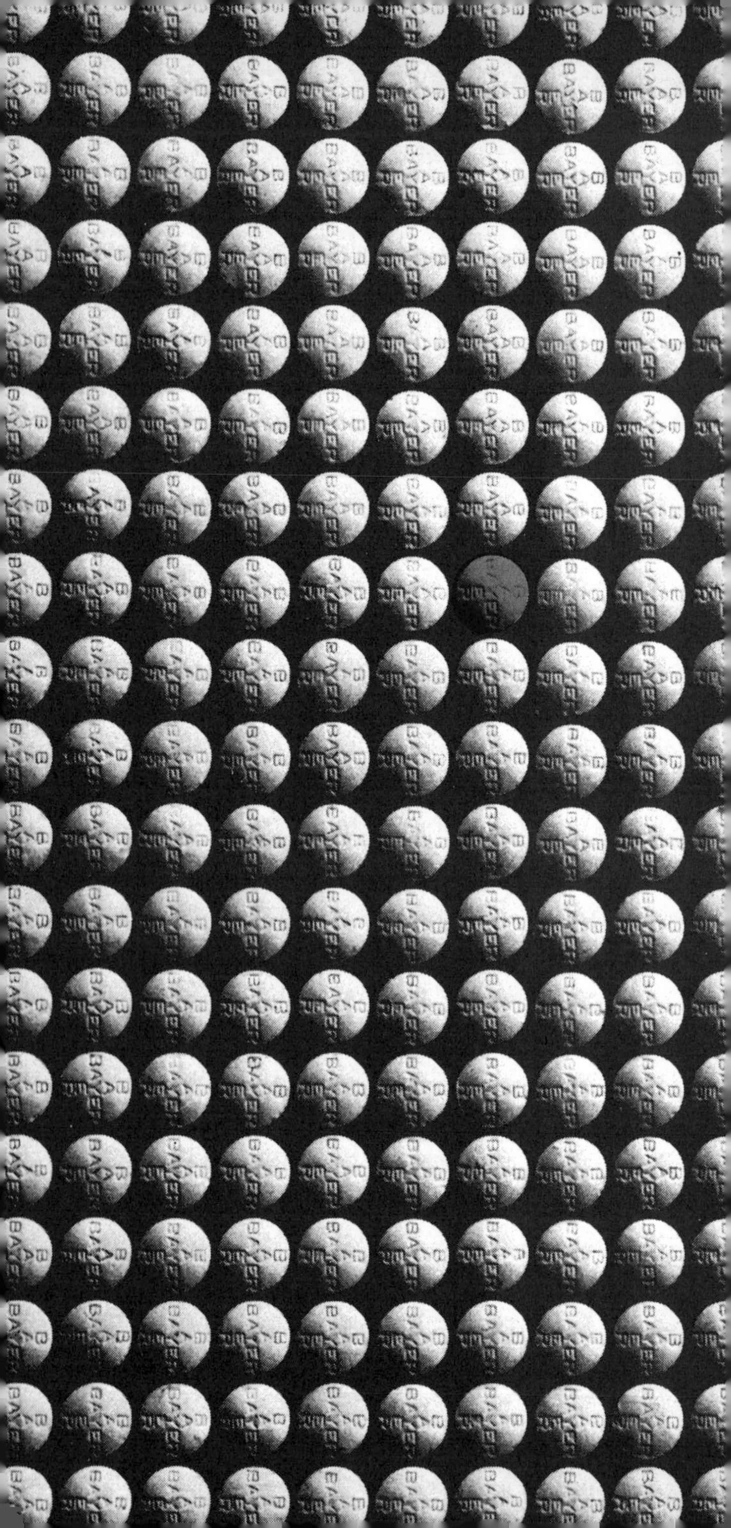
BAYER

BAYER

BAYER

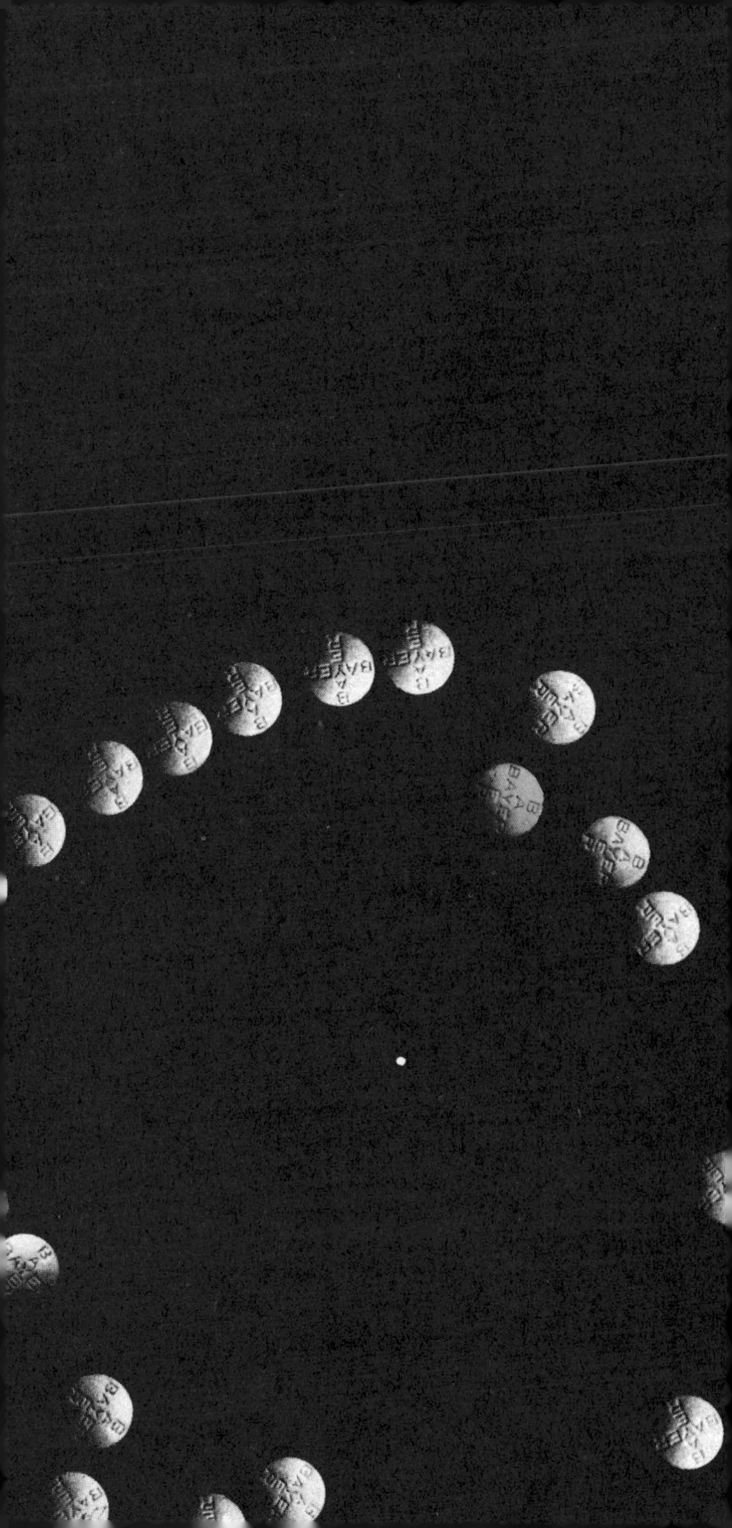

RAH

RAH

THEY FOUGHT AND WON BATTLES OVER CITIES
AND RECALLED IT TO THEIR GRANDCHILDREN
great AS YAHWEH'S VICTORY

hey DON'T GET THE IDEA THEY WERE SOME KIND
OF FOOLS piously CREDITING YAHWEH FOR
THINGS THEY DID THEMSELVES

YAHWEH REALLY DID ALL THAT STUFF really

OTHER PEOPLE'S HISTORY BOOKS MIGHT HAVE MENTIONED THE SAME THINGS AND EXPLAINED THEM WITH quite SECULAR WORDS they told it like it was

BUT THE HEBREWS' HISTORY SAID LISTEN THAT MIGHT LOOK just plain SECULAR BUT LOOKS ARE DECEIVING

IT WAS YAHWEH AT WORK ALL IS HIS GIFT good

so THEY CELEBRATED THEIR ANNIVERSARIES AROUND THE TABLE CHILDREN ON GRANDPA'S LAP GIVING SPECIAL MEANINGS TO SPECIAL EVENTS OR PEOPLE OR THINGS OR PLACES OR TIMES

RAH!
RAH!
RAH!

BUT NOT JUST DOING IT FOR THE SAKE OF DOING IT for fun BUT SO THINGS SORTED OUT AND NAMED SPECIAL COULD BECOME SIGNS by which TO SEE REGULAR THINGS IN NEW WAYS DAILY NEWS AS GOOD NEWS if you please

i dig the shape of the news the news is where it's happening

EVERY TIME THEY TURNED AROUND SOMETHING place time body HELPED THEM REMEMBER WHO WHAT WHEN WHERE WHY THEY WERE that's important they said

LIFE WAS A SIGN stop and go OF GOOD YAHWEH'S GOOD PRESENCE

IT WAS EASY TO SAY YES WITH SO MUCH HELP so they said it yes

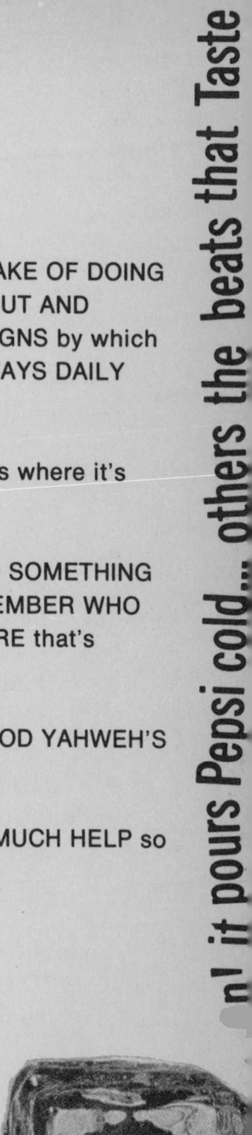

RoyaL Des
Tuna
Instant Drink fa
Sea
Chicken
Tang
Prunes &
Raisins y Del
Cerealsisss
of the Nabisco
Monte
Coffeeu

MAYBE WE SHOULDN'T SPEND SO MUCH
TIME
IN DAYS GONE BY bye BUT
IT ALL SEEMS TO
HAVE STARTED BACK THERE for us at least

THAT BUNCH IS STILL AROUND it seems
BIGGER BUNCH MORE
DIVERSE DECENTRALIZED
and all BUT STILL AROUND

WITH EVEN MORE holy HISTORY
TO REMEMBER
the number of years is bigger

Kraft Cheese

t Break

AND BY ALL MEANS MORE
holy HISTORY TO OFFER
more things and people and times
and events today than ever before IN
WHICH TO KNOW GOD'S PRESENCE
and see him

AND WE STILL EAT OUR
FRIENDLY MEALS with
friends and all
IN ORDER TO REMEMBER WHO
WHAT WHEN WHERE WHY
and even how old WE
ARE

THE SPECIALEST MEALS REMEMBER
for us THE MOST
IMPORTANT QUESTIONS
notice the word
is questions not answers

Birds Eye Vegetables Hormel Meat

Chase & Sborn

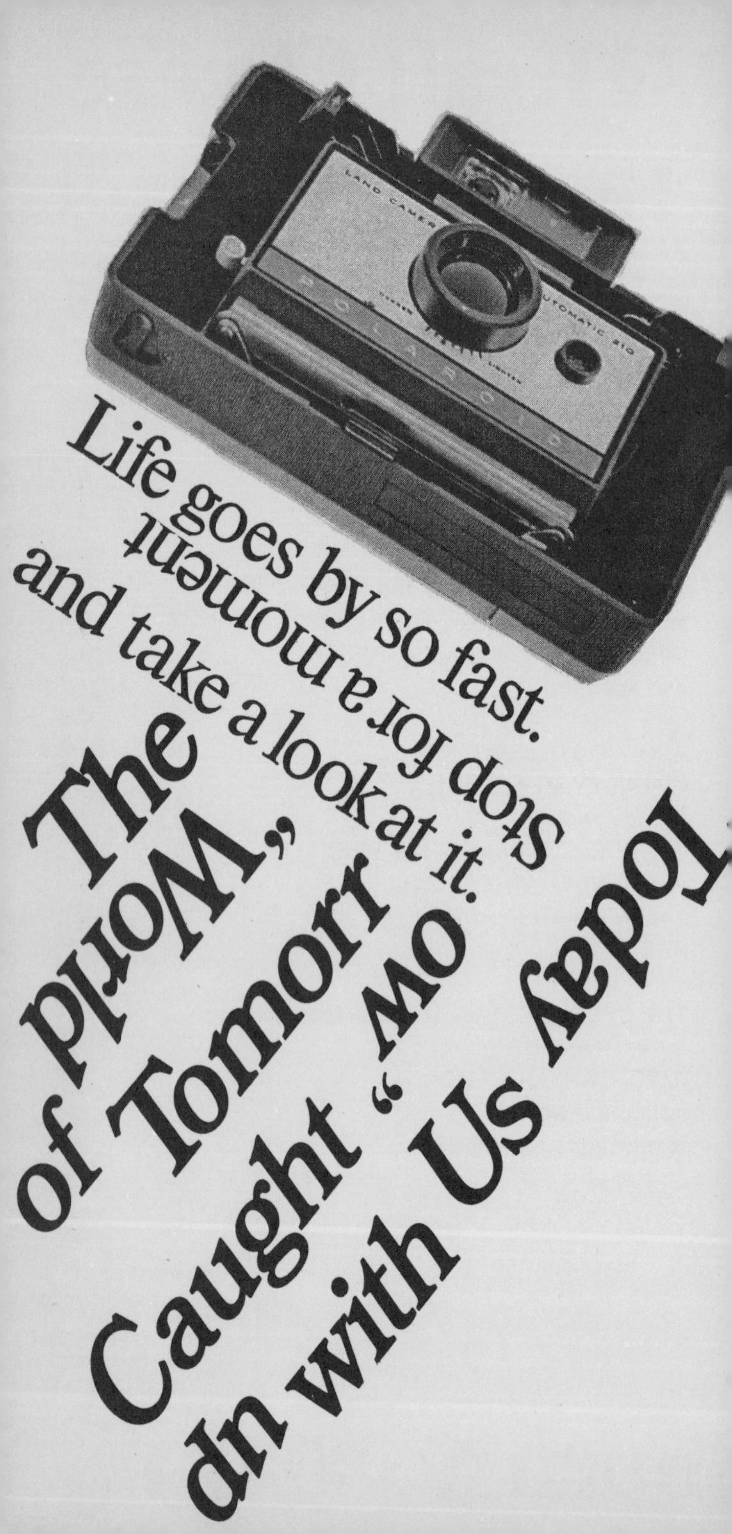
POLAROID
Life goes by so fast.
Stop for a moment
and take a look at it.
The "World of Tomorrow"
Caught up with Us Today.

WE GROUP TO EAT AND DRINK AND IN OUR EATING AND DRINKING AFFIRM WHAT WE SAID IN THE FIRST PLACE heaven and earth weren't meant to be a world apart

HEAVEN AND EARTH AREN'T A WORLD APART

GOD HIMSELF HAS ENTERED INTO THE WORLD
HEAVEN IS PRESENT AMONG MEN

what we mean is JESUS IS CHRIST IS JESUS

WE daringly CALL OUR BREAD it builds strong bodies rejoices man's heart AND WINE JESUS' BODY AND BLOOD SAYING BY THAT HE IS PRESENT PERSONALLY HERE REALLY AND BODILY

come to where the flavor is

WHY ARE SOME PEOPLE FAT AND PEOPLE SKINNY?

of course IT COULD BE AN UNUSUAL quite MEAL no table a little sip of sweet wine a taste of pressed bread being fed and all

BUT IT COULD BE much more A GOOD WAY TO SEE ALL OUR EATING watermelon del monte canned foods pizza AND DRINKING wet & wild beat others cold taste with twice the bubbles

BESIDES A WAY OF LOOKING even AT METRECAL THE HUNGRY $2/3$ ALKA SELTZER SUNKIST SKINNY PEOPLE PICNICS and CHASE AND SANBORN COFFEE besides

Christmas

Instant

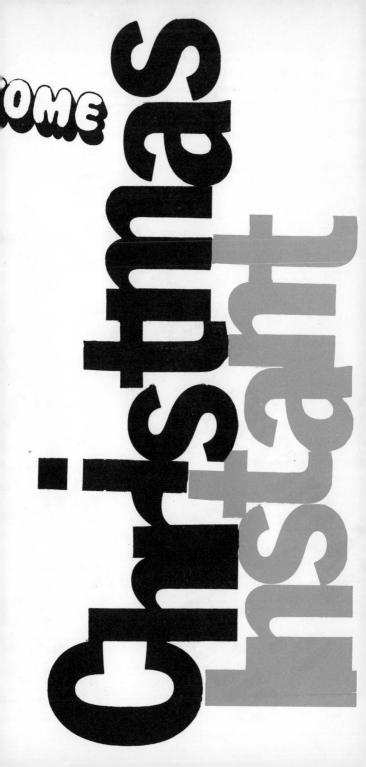

OME

IT COULD BE A QUAINT LITTLE CEREMONY TO HELP US REMEMBER A SPECIAL EVENT that's nice enough

Come to Marlboro Country

The Longhorns

YOU'VE GOT THINGS GOING FOR YOU

For people who are afraid to say it out loud

OR IT COULD more more BE A FRESH WAY TO LOOK AT ALL CURRENT EVENTS RUNNING gas hauler's strike 1984 soft lunar landing world war i ii iii rolled mustang china bomb graduation the alarm clock just went off it's time to get up and get going

more more more IT COULD BE A nice WAY OF REMEMBERING ALL ABOUT ONE MAN NAMED JESUS good idea

OR MAYBE A WAY OF REMEMBERING ALL MEN CALLED JESUS or judas or jose or john or jim jan joan jerry jean jacques joe jennifer

HONK

HONK

or even those beginning with a or m or z for that matter zorba

AND BY CALLING THEIR NAMES REMEMBERING IF THEY ARE FAT OR CRABBY OR SICK OR BLACK OR HUNGRY OR PRETTY OR HAPPY or need you to call them today

IT COULD BE A TIME TO CAPTURE ANOTHER TIME LONG TIME AGO the night he was betrayed before he died the good time at suppertime with friends far spent time ETC

but then again IT COULD BE A WAY OF PUTTING YOUR FINGER ON ALL TIME good times bad times rotten times high times old times party times new york times special times any time

some other guy will
want it just as
much as you
do now.

things
really
changed

IT COULD BE THE MENTAL RECONSTRUCTION OF A PLACE apart UPPER ROOM JERUSALEM not far from GOLGOTHA BETHLEHEM or even NAZARETH

OR IT COULD BECOME THE NAMING OF NAMES OF ALL PLACES selma watts new york vietnam fremont denver grand canyon nagasaki riverview park church auschwitz grandma's house home room home HE LIVES AND DIES

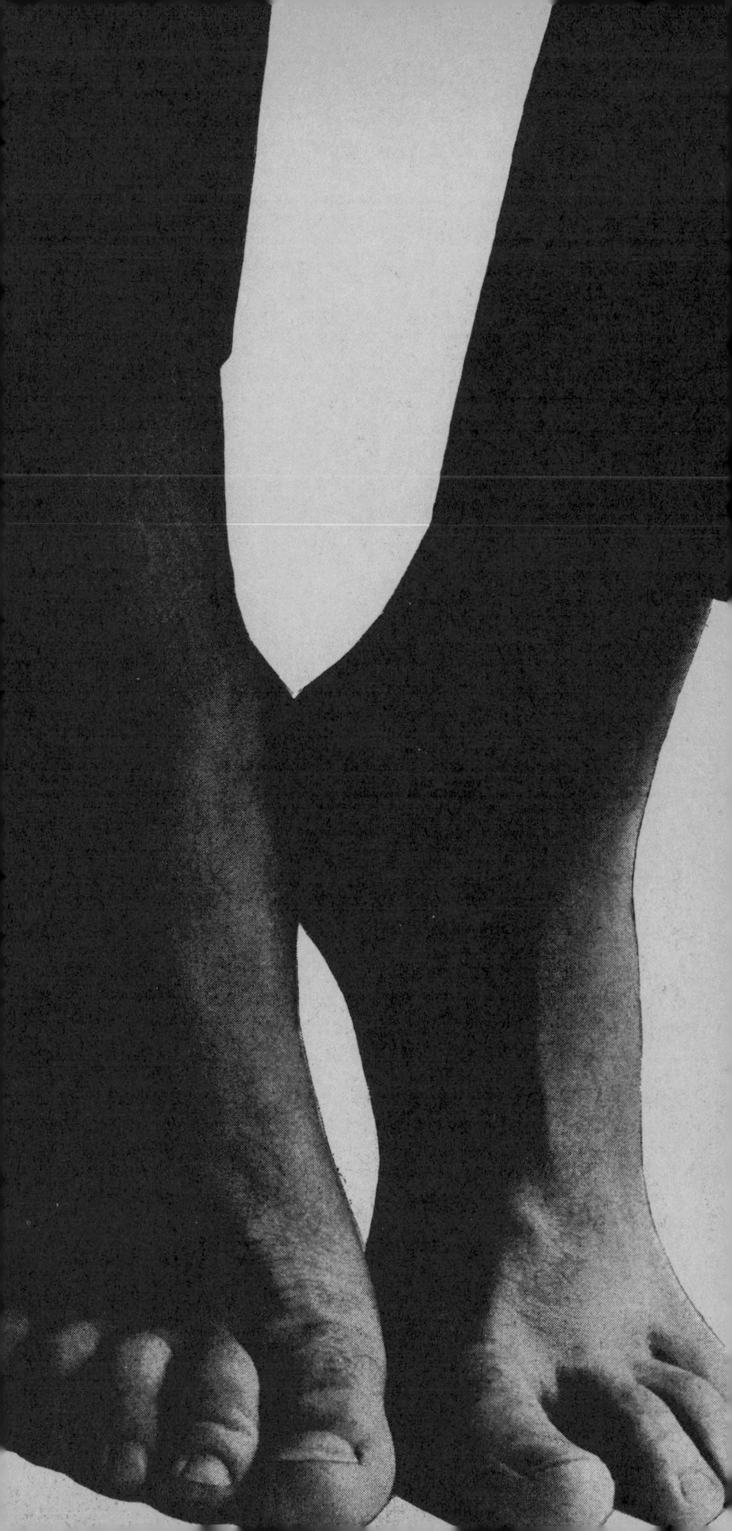

THERE ARE LOTS OF WAYS OF LOOKING AT OUR HISTORY WE'RE NOT TRYING TO BE EXCLUSIVE

JUST MAKE SURE THE WAY YOU CHOOSE personal viewing DOESN'T GET YOU SO HUNG UP ON THE PAST YOU CAN'T SEE IT AS A SIGN FOR UNDERSTANDING THE PRESENT and pushing you into the future

THAT'S WHAT'S GOOD ABOUT THE EUCHARIST IT'S PAST PRESENT FUTURE we are asked to remember TODAY his death YESTERDAY until he comes TOMORROW

ood thing a
LIFE
Christmas
gift doesn't
arrive
all at once.
t would

ALL ROLLED INTO ONE

good to know

BECAUSE PASTS HAVE A TENDENCY terrible TO PULL PEOPLE DOWN INTO THEM like so much quicksand

SOMETIMES WE DON'T LIKE THAT one little bit ESPECIALLY IF THE PIECE OF PAST WE'RE ASKED TO VALUE LACKS VALUE but that's the way we've always done it

i never got by with that

AND FUTURES in like fashion HAVE A WAY OF DEMANDING TOO MUCH OF OUR ENERGIES AND THOUGHTS

lives are rooted rutted insured shored up protected invested securitied planned fenced in willed landscaped DOES TODAY EXIST FOR TOMORROW OR TODAY

consider the lilies of the field poor solomon

THE cybernetic rendezvous FUTURE IS MOST EXCITING no question about it BUT ITS FIERCE UNCERTAINTIES COMPEL US NOT TO PUT ALL OUR EGGS IN ONE that BASKET

wild new ways
to get that old feeling.

It’s a whole
game. new
ball
Voilà.

it
can
be
a
ho

YOUNG PEOPLE HAVE BEEN CALLED THE NOW GENERATION time MOST PEOPLE THINK THAT'S A BAD WORD just you wait

DON'T BE SO SURE maybe FORCED TO FIND MEANING IN THE NOW PRESENT MOMENT to say yes to it HAS ALWAYS BEEN ASKED OF US we haven't been listening too well

PAST AND FUTURE TUG AWAY AT EACH OTHER BOTH WANTING US FOR THEIR VERY OWN

WHERE THEY MEET IN TENSION IS NOW right here and now

IT'S EASIER they say TO LIVE THE MOMENT how can anyone agree

from old

young

Will today's news affect your investments?

mobile.

IT'S THE ROUGHEST we insist BECAUSE IT'S THE POINT OF TENSION it's easier to live in past or future you see you don't have to contend with decisions decisions decisions they're ready made to order

IT'S WHERE THE ACTION IS and that's not always as fun wet & wild as it sounds either

perhaps NOW IS THE ACCEPTABLE TIME to quote a friend

NOW IS WHEN HE'S PRESENT remember

Just getting there will be like shooting a bee in flight with an air rifle from a whirling merry-go-round at a range of 100 yards.

Getting back will be even tougher.

Coke
TRADE-MARK®
Coca-Cola
TRADE MARK ®

SO hey DON'T LET IT SLIP BETWEEN YOUR FINGERS CUP YOUR HANDS or something AND DRINK IT ALL IN

open up an orange and taste the sunshine sunkist from california-arizona

TASTE GOD AND SEE THAT HE IS GOOD BETTER BEST offer him a sip

PERHAPS OUR SPECIAL GLANCES AT HISTORY END UP BEING REHEARSALS FOR THE FINE ART OF SEEING GOD ALIVE TODAY do you still doubt that he is

HAVING LEARNED imperfectly HOW HE COMES TO MAN the initial shock of knowing he comes in tap chlorined water dictionary words poorly constructed people that eat drink sleep curse laugh cry die bread builds strong wonder bodies 12 ways wine from the corner liquor store in a brown bag events that sometimes usually don't make the newspapers may be too much DISGUISED in with and under

WE BEGIN TO LOOK FOR THE CLUES AND SIGNS methodically we probe the hidden depths of the daily news WHOSE SIDE IS HE ON

is that the right question WE INSIST AND WHEN WE KNOW IT'S NOT THE RIGHT QUESTION WE SEE HIM IN THE CENTER where the action is

he's the peacemaker that much we know maybe reconcile rings a bell

Correct Correct

Correct

Maybe they know ing

don't know someth

you

Correct Correct

Fascinating!

HE MAY though BE THERE protesting ANGRY there are some things he doesn't like any more than we do SHALL WE JOIN HIM THERE

if we're convinced he's there maybe we should

PERHAPS HE LIKES THE SHAPE OF THE NEWS and he's invited angels to sing and dance

THINK HE WOULD MIND IF WE DANCED TOO i don't

HALF
PRICE

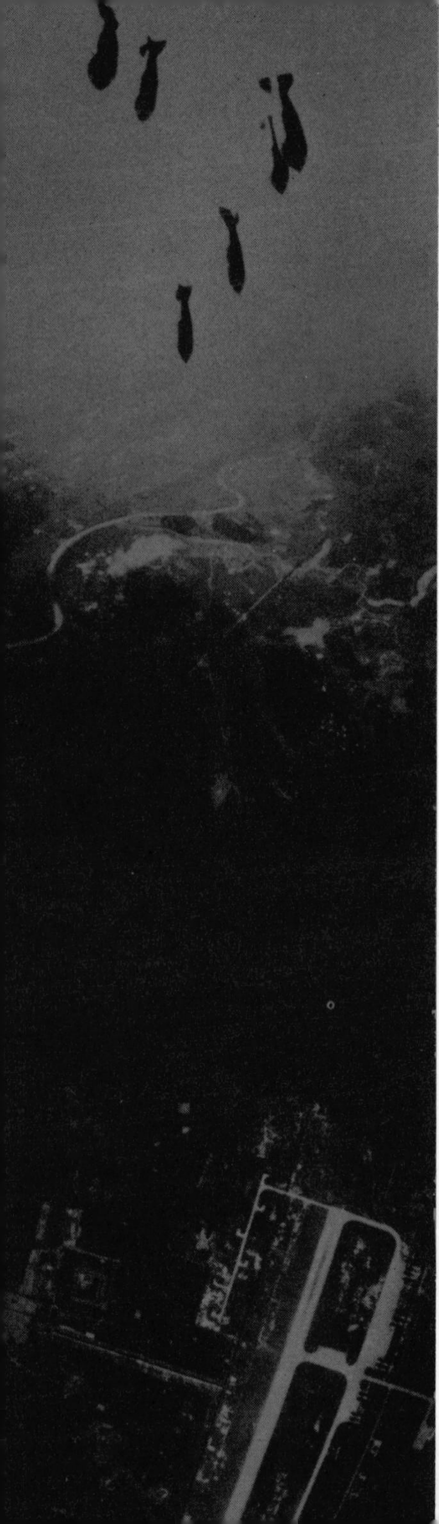

¿

Maybe
diet flo
becaus
ate the

OR MAYBE HE'S SO BUSY WORKING
here or there
so deeply involved
HE HASN'T HAD TIME FOR
A CUP OF COFFEE
bring on the java
how about some service
WHILE YOU'RE UP
WHY DON'T YOU GIVE A HAND

HE TEACHES US WELL

WE ARE SOON CONVINCED
OUR EQUIPMENT IS
ADEQUATE FOR THE JOB

'our last
ped
'ou
vrong breakfast.

The closer he gets...

to Disneyland.

Can anything this beautiful

Take your mother

the better you look!

really be a tiger?

OUR MAJOR CELEBRATING HAS TAUGHT US HOW TO CELEBRATE birthdays school's out cokes sweater that turns them on miniskirt the keys you name it AND OUR MINOR CELEBRATINGS KEEP US IN SHAPE FOR OUR MAJOR ONES

WH RE

AT'S ALHA

LY P

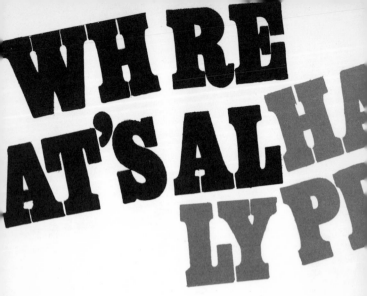

OUR SENSORS ARE SHARPENED SIGNS APPEAR EVERYWHERE FROM OUT OF NOWHERE 1400 ads a day say more than buy buy buy sounds get better by the disc you can feel the shape of the news it's deeper than wide this year people need people it's as simple as that anything this beautiful has got to be a tiger

RUN FOR YOUR LIFE THE HILLS ARE ALIVE WITH THE SOUND OF MUSIC

ENI
NG

you have at least nine months to live perhaps as
many as 18 i haven't taken a day off since law school
guess i'll have to squeeze 30 years of living into one
or maybe two

AND WE DANCE IN THE MIDST OF ABSURDITY

WE HAVE NO CHOICE have we

IN A WORLD THAT GOES TO BED HUNGRY
400000000 starve 2300000000 go hungry 20000 die
DAILY IF THEY HAVE A BED OR EVER GET TO IT

HOW ACCEPT THE GIFT OF FATNESS

Win a smashing, dashing, glittering, glamorous

IN A WORLD THAT CLASSES VIOLENCE AN ACCEPTABLE MODE OF GAINING ITS ENDS 500000 civilian vietnamese women and children robbed of homes can't be wrong the mafia runs loose

kill for peace

HOW ACKNOWLEDGE THE GIFT OF PEACE

IN A WORLD ⅔ NONWHITE colorful some prefer to be named CONTROLLED BY WHITE

HOW SEE THE HUMAN RACE

A

IN A WORLD OF SHEER UNCERTAINTY ABOUT TOMORROW sometimes today even some tinker toys are nuclear jobs don't exist that today's 1st graders will fill in 20 years crossing streets is dangerous

HOW HAVE HOPE or anything of that sort HOW CELEBRATE LIFE

HOW DANCE AND SING AND EAT GOOD FOOD AND SLEEP AND LAUGH AND RUN AND SAY YES AND WEAR BRIGHT ORANGE

every week!

Make the most of their
"Wonder Years"

NESS
TOGETHER
SUPER

AAAAHHHHH THAT'S THE BEAUTY OF THE BEAST we shout in instant replay HOW DARE WE NOT SAY YES snoopy knows

FOR A GOD WHO LAUGHS AT OPEN TOMBS HAS GOT THE WHOLE BIT IN HIS HANDS i wanna hold your hand

IT'S HIS BABY deny it disbelieve it hide from it anything you like YOU CAN'T ESCAPE IT

People need help from people; it's as simple as that

SURE GET INVOLVED
GET LOST
GIVE YOURSELF AWAY
DIE GIVING LIFE

BECAUSE
THAT'S ONLY HALF
THE NAME OF THE GAME

LIVE IN DYING
GET IN
GIVING AWAY
FIND YOURSELF
IN GETTING LOST
BE FREE
BY GETTING INVOLVED

Tell them how you had to walk
five miles to school in the snow

enough to have a Rover 2000
T.C. Sports Sedan ();
and that your every waking
thought, yours and mommy's,
is of them, and all you are
working for is to give them
the advantages you never

now the game's name's complete hope you still recognize it with its new name and rules

ACCEPT THE GIFT OF FATNESS BY HELPING SKINNY PEOPLE GET FAT who wants to get fat i do so do a lot of other people

AND BE GLAD YOU'RE FAT by the way

ACKNOWLEDGE THE GIFT OF PEACE BY GIVING IT AWAY kiss of peace it used to be called in the eucharist keep it in one piece

AND DON'T FORGET TO SLEEP WELL rest in peace

The harder they try,

the better

This is where you come when you're through playing games.

We get.

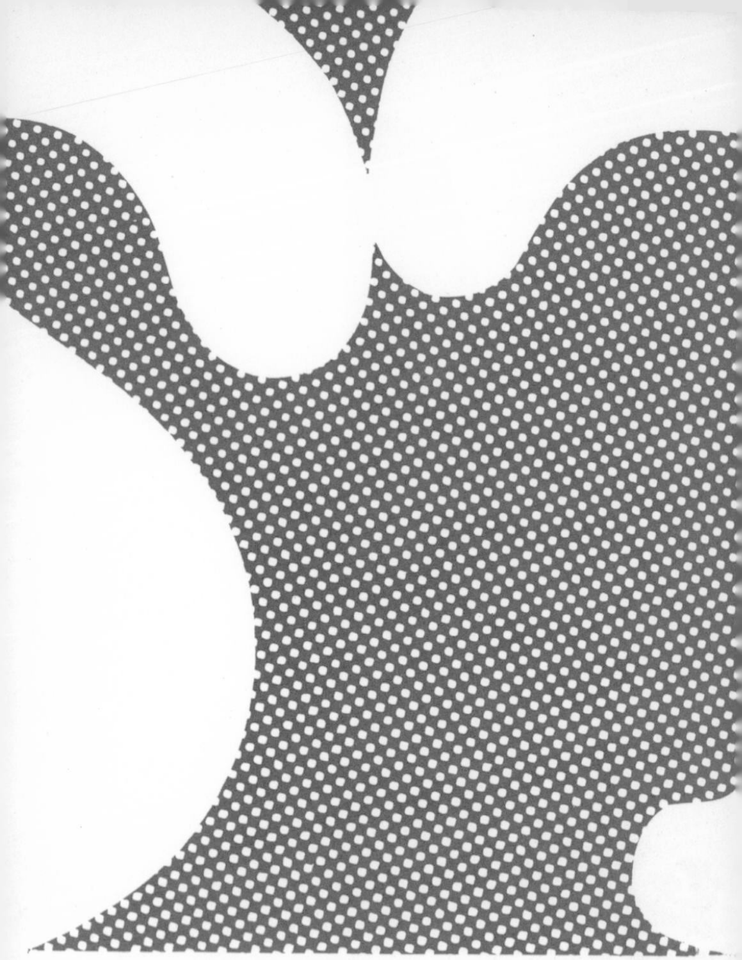

SEE THE WHOLE HUMAN RACE BY ENJOYING ITS DAZZLING COLORFULNESS nbc has nothing on us peacock

oh yes SHOUT LOUD THAT BLACK IS BEAUTIFUL BABY and so is white and yellow and red and all the various shades thereof in between

'DODGE fever

HAVE HOPE BY WORKING LIKE ALL GET OUT TO
GET THAT BUTTON IN YOUR HAND THAT DECISION
IN YOUR DEPARTMENT A STOP AND GO LIGHT ON
YOUR CORNER what do you say

THE EUCHARIST INSISTS

AND THEN REMEMBER THAT THE TOMB IS EMPTY yours that is AND THAT HE'S COMING

THROW THAT INTO THE TEETH OF A WORLD LIKE THIS

THEN SIT BACK AND ENJOY THE FIREWORKS

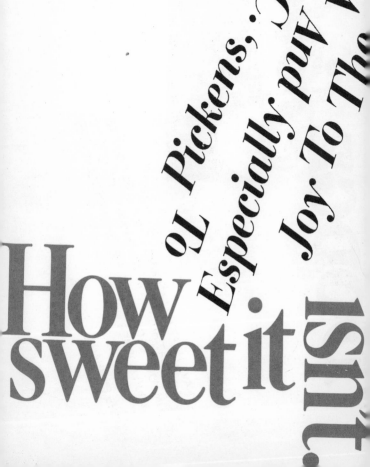

YES

To Pickens, S.C.
Especially And
Joy To The World!

How sweet it isn't!

Send me 33 weeks
of TIME and bill
me for $3.97
Miss
Mrs.
Mr.
Name
Address
City
(please print)
gnature
State
ollege student, please indicate: ☐ undergraduate ☐ graduate
Zip Code
e of College/University
Year Studies End
ood just in U.S. and Canada. New subscribers only.
T 4129